CONTINUOUSLY DELIVERING JAVASCRIPT TO AWS WITH GITHUB

Quickly and efficiently getting your application on the cloud

TABLE OF CONTENTS

ABOUT THE AUTHOR

I am Shane Preater, a software consultant and mentor with over 20 years' experience.

I have worked with many large international companies to help them to identify and correct issues with their software systems. This has included creating large scale systems from scratch as well as helping to redesign / modify systems to better fit their needs.

With an expertise in various development languages including: Java, Python and JavaScript, I have provided training and mentoring to groups of developers from individuals to large organization levels.

Back in 2015 I started to provide more DevOps based solutions to my clients. This included setting up entire containerized solutions on their premises using tools like Kubernetes and Docker swarm but, also creating full solutions using both AWS and Azure.

I specialize in helping my clients to fix problems in both their software solutions and also their software development process. Helping them to streamline their process and improve the quality and maintainability of their codebases.

Although my life as a software developer started with something of a bump, originally, I was working as a Chemist and doing a degree in chemistry when I broke my leg whilst doing martial arts. This sounds exciting, maybe it was breaking logs with my bare feet, or possibly it was during a sparring match, alas no, it was while doing sprints during the warm up. I managed to turn wrong and came down heavily on my ankle fracturing the bone. This meant I had all the inconvenience of 6 – 8 weeks of healing but no cast or any sympathy. During this time I was living with my parents, so my mum bought me a "Sam's: Teach yourself C in 21 days" book to keep me occupied. I like to think this was because she was keen for me to expand my horizons and she knew I had a love for computers and tech. Although partially true, the main reason was to shut up my moaning about being house bound and bored. This book struck a chord with me and I devoured it within the week. I was then off writing small programs and generally getting obsessed with programming. I then got the "Sam's: Teach yourself C++ in 21 days" book to further expand my knowledge. Once this was completed, I started to send out my resume to everyone and everybody I could find. 10 months later I was given a single interview at a company the other end of the country from where I was living. Again, my mum came to my aid and said she would come with me for the interview so she could keep me company. I got the job and had a month to find accommodation and move out from my parents and that was the moment that my life changed forever.

INTRODUCTION

Open web is something that has allowed people to share their creativity online for years. Let's think back on how computer science operated only a couple of decades ago to what we have now. The change is astronomical. Not only is so much of our society intertwined with technology, but software development is no longer something only a few partake in. The world of software development is expanding, making so much possible and with this comes the ability to share your information with others.

Let's take a service like GitHub. You now have a central (and free) location for your source code. This means the storage of data is not maintained by you or your company. Gone are the days of needing to back up your work on an external drive such as a floppy disk, CD, or even a USB drive. Also, as this is a central resource on the web, you as a developer, have much easier access to contribute and work on that codebase.

Next you have cloud services; this again means you don't need to own and maintain your own infrastructure stacks. You can simply spin up resources as required and then stop them when done. Amazon Web Services (AWS) is one such provider. They offer a whole host of services to streamline and simplify the process of developing and running systems. To go through their whole offering is beyond the scope of this book so we will focus on only the relevant services to get our deployment process up and running.

There has been a shift in recent years away from the "waterfall" style approach to developing systems. Gone are the days where you have a separate team to perform each of the vital tasks when creating a software solution. Before you would have specific coders, testers and then infrastructure engineers. These days it's more efficient to run your software development teams as DevOps teams. This means that the team is responsible for the development, testing and deployment of the software solution. All made possible by the introduction of better testing frameworks and tools. One of the biggest enablers to this rapid style of development is the continuous integration and continuous delivery process (CI/CD). This process allows for code to be written, tested and deployed using as autonomous a process as practicable.

CI/CD is basically two parts to a whole. First we have CI or continuous integration. To quote Thought Works here:

> *Continuous Integration (CI) is a development practice that requires developers to integrate code into a shared repository several times a day. Each check-in is then verified by an automated build, allowing teams to detect problems early.*
>
> - *Thought Works (https://www.thoughtworks.com/ continuous-integration)*

This is saying that we can decrease the time spent on defects and bugs by integrating early and often.

Then we have the second part CD or Continuous delivery (or deployment depending on which websites you use).

To quote the continuous delivery website now:

> *Continuous Delivery is the ability to get changes of all types—including new features, configuration changes, bug fixes and experiments—into production, or into the hands of users, safely and quickly in a sustainable way.*
>
> - *https://continuousdelivery.com/*

This means that we are getting from development to having our code in production in the shortest time possible. This greatly enhances the users engagement and quick feedback.

Making use of cloud services like AWS will help us to enable the CI/CD process. We can therefore setup our development process so that when we commit a change to the repository, it will automatically perform the following steps:

1. Build the newly committed assets.
2. Run the tests, ensuring they pass.
3. Package the code up ready for deployment.
4. Deploy the code.

In this book, we will walk through each of the steps required to get a JavaScript based application up and running on AWS using the tools described above.

If you would like to follow along with this process but do not have your own code then you can use the code from this book at https://github.com/shanepreater/javascript-on-aws . The best way to use this is to fork the repository, which is described later.

CREATING A GITHUB ACCOUNT

GitHub is a popular tool for people to store their source code. No matter what you are working on, whether it be a website or a backend system, no matter the coding language; you can put it on GitHub to store. Not only that, but GitHub acts as a portfolio for coders to send to prospective employers and clients.

This a Git backed version control system. What this means is that a programmer can work on the code base locally and at various points during their development they can "commit" sets of changes. The set of changes, or changeset, is stored as the difference of what the codebase looked like before and what it looks like now. After committing their code, the programmer can then "Push" those changes to the central repository. It's only at the point when the programmer pushes, that their code is available outside of their local development machine.

Git also allows a programmer to "branch" their work so that they can make bigger changes with multiple commits but that don't affect the main codebase straight away. This is really useful when working on bigger features, or when you want to get testing and assurances of new code before unleashing it upon your customers. When the branch has been completed and the quality assured, this can then be merged back to the main branch ready to be delivered to the customers. The normal workflow for merging these "feature" branches is to create a "Pull request" or PR. This PR can then be reviewed by the programmer's peers, have the tests run and confirm they pass and also have any automated quality assurance processes run prior to the PR being approved and the code merged. This code flow is illustrated and explained in more detail at https://guides.github.com/introduction/flow/.

In order to make use of GitHub, you are going to need an account. Setting up an account is very easy and straight forward.

Navigate to https://github.com. This will present you with the sign up box:

Username

Email

Password

Make sure it's at least 15 characters OR at least 8 characters including a number and a lowercase letter. Learn more.

Sign up for GitHub

By clicking "Sign up for GitHub", you agree to our Terms of Service and Privacy Statement. We'll occasionally send you account related emails.

1 - GitHub Sign up dialog

Simply fill in your details in the provided boxes

You will then be required to verify your account. GitHub has a neat little puzzle that you need to "solve" in order to prove you are a real person.

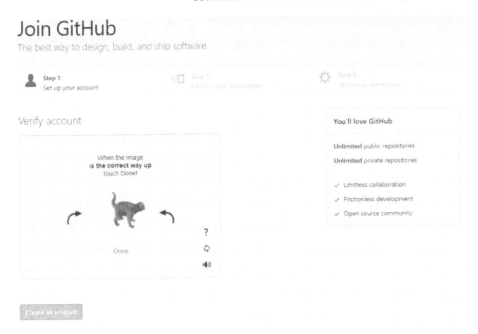

2 - GitHub Verification puzzle

Once this has been completed you will need to decide the type of account you require. There are currently two options:

1. Free: This provides both public and private repositories but has limited support for multiple contributors.
2. Pro: This has all the benefits but also costs a monthly subscription.

You will then have some questions to answer in order to help personalize your experience.

Finally you will need to verify the email address that you provided in the first step.

CREATING A REPOSITORY ON GITHUB

In order to store your project on GitHub, you are going to need to create a repository. How do you go about creating a repository, you might be asking? This is what we will be covering in this chapter:

Once again navigate to https://github.com

On any page, click the plus (+) sign on the upper right hand corner. A drop down menu will then appear and you will then click the "New repository" option:

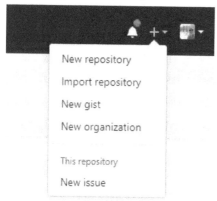

3 - GitHub Add dropdown

Choose a short name for your repository. In the example, I have used "javascript-on-aws".

You can then write a description about your repository. This is an optional step, but something you should do in order to properly track what you are doing.

Then choose to make the repository private or public. This is pretty straight forward, but the purpose of this option is to either have it public where anyone can access your project, or private so only you or those you share with can see it.

The next step would be to click the option **Initialize this repository with a README**.

If you want you can pick one of the licenses to have with your repository.

The last step is to then click the "Create repository" button.

Create a new repository

A repository contains all project files, including the revision history. Already have a project repository elsewhere? Import a repository.

Owner   Repository name *

shanepreater ▾   /

Great repository names are short and memorable. Need inspiration? How about friendly-robot?

Description (optional)

◉ Public
   Anyone can see this repository. You choose who can commit.

○ Private
   You choose who can see and commit to this repository.

Skip this step if you're importing an existing repository.

☐ Initialize this repository with a README
   This will let you immediately clone the repository to your computer.

Add .gitignore: None ▾   Add a license: None ▾   ⓘ

Create repository

4 - GitHub New repository dialog

As you can see, that was incredibly easy.

Sometimes, when we think of coding, we can get intimidated about it. This, though is an easy process. The steps may seem tedious, but it's easy to do. Keep in mind that the README files are the files for you to describe your project in more details. These RE-ADME files are at the front page of your repository.

If you are changing a single file then you can commit a change to your repository directly in the GitHub UI. What is a commit? it's a snapshot of all of your files in the project at a certain time.

How do you commit a change in your README file? Look below.

Click on the README.md option in your repository's list of files.

Above the file's content, then click the "edit" option in the form of the pen/pencil symbol.

5 - The edit icon

Click on the edit file tab and type information in about yourself.

Click the "preview changes" option above the new content.

Review the changes you made. Green changes are new items and Red are removed items.

Scroll to the bottom to see the commit dialog

6 - The commit changes form

You can type a short, meaningful message in the first box (GitHub will provide a default for you). This will describe the change you made. You can also add a longer description of what you changed, and why, in the text box.

You will want to decide whether you want to add your commit to the current branch or a new branch below the commit message fields. Typically, when developing software, you would contribute your various changes to a branch before creating a pull request to get the code reviewed and merged into the master. For this example, though we can simply commit to master.

You then will click "Commit changes".

If you follow these steps, you will be able to easily create a repository and commit a change.

FORKING AN EXISTING REPOSITORY

Another of the benefits of GitHub, is the ease with which you can take some existing work and then modify it for your own specific needs. This process is called forking. It basically involves you creating a copy of the original work and then creating a repository from that.

In this chapter we will fork the example repository that was created to accompany this book.

Navigate to the correct GitHub repository at https://github.com/shanepreater/javascript-on-aws

In the top right you will see a button marked fork, click this.

That is all you need to do. You will now have a copy of the repository in your repositories.

This chapter has shown how trivial it is to use an existing project as the basis to begin your development repository. This is one of the major benefits of using GitHub for your code storage.

CREATING A FREE AWS ACCOUNT

As stated earlier, AWS stands for Amazon Web Services. This is one of the biggest providers of cloud services. Their offerings include virtual servers, load balancing, machine learning, data storage, databases and much, much more.

Follow the steps below to create a free AWS account:

You will want to go to the https://aws.amazon.com/ home page.

If you have not previously signed in to AWS, you will click the "Create an AWS Account". If you have already signed in beforehand there may be an option for "Sign into the Console" which is located in the top right.

You will be presented with the sign up dialog:

Create an AWS account

Email address

[   ]

Password

[   ]

Confirm password

[   ]

AWS account name ⓘ

[   ]

[Continue   ]

Sign in to an existing AWS account

7 - AWS sign up form

Enter the correct information needed before clicking "Continue". If you do not see "Create an AWS Account" then you may have to click "Sign into a different account" before then clicking on "Create an AWS Account".

You will then be presented with the contact information page:

Please select the account type and complete the fields below with your contact details.

Account type ℹ

○ Professional   ◉ Personal

Full name

[   ]

Phone number

[   ]

Country/Region

[United States   ▼]

Address

[Street, P.O. Box, Company Name, c/o]

[Apartment, suite, unit, building, floor, etc.]

City

[   ]

State / Province or region

[   ]

Postal code

[   ]

☐ Check here to indicate that you have read
   and agree to the terms of the AWS
   Customer Agreement

[Create Account and Continue   ]

8 - AWS Contact details from

Account type has two options, while they both offer the same features and functions, you are still going to have to choose one of them.

Of course, there is an AWS Agreement clause that you will have to read and agree to.

Finally, choose "Create Account and Continue".

After you are done with those steps, there are a few other things that you will have to do when setting up your free AWS account.

Add a payment plan via the "Payment Information" page. After doing this, click the button that says, "Secure Submit".

Verify your phone number.

Choose to verify your phone number either by text message or voice call.

Then choose your country code or your region code from the list provided.

Enter a phone number for a phone that is nearby so you can verify your phone number.

Enter the code that is provided via captcha.

Choose the "Contact me" option that will send you that verification code in the way that you have chosen.

Enter a pin and then hit "Continue".

Choose an AWS support plan.

Wait for your AWS account to be activated!

Please keep in mind that activation could take up to 24 hours, so don't fret if your account is not activated right away!

HOW TO INSTALL JENKINS ON EC2

What is Jenkins? Jenkins is an open-source automation software that is primarily used to provide continuous integration and delivery of your software.

Jenkins was originally called Hudson, and was developed by Sun Microsystems in 2004. This was generally considered to be a better alternative to Cruise Control. It was renamed Jenkins in 2011.

So, how do you spin up an instance of Jenkins?

Jenkins is designed as a distributed service. This makes it very scalable for all sizes of organization. Jenkins has two main components: The server, this is where the main work of Jenkins is configured and instigated. The slave, these are workers which perform the steps necessary in building and testing newly developed code.

First, we need to create the Jenkins server. For this, you will want to use the Amazon Elastic Compute Cloud aka EC2. You will want to have access to this from the "public" internet, rather than just within your Amazon account. Amazon has two concepts for this: "Virtual Private Cloud" or VPC, this is your own private area that is only accessible to you, or anyone you have provided login credentials. Then there is a "public subnet", this is a route for web addresses that are publicly accessible to reach your VPC virtual machines. Don't worry too much about this as Amazon has streamlined these concepts so you will quickly get the hang of it.

There is another important concept when using AWS that needs to be understood. "Identity Access Management" or IAM. This is the security layer that Amazon have made available to ensure that you can protect who has access to your virtual resources, and, what they can do with them. It is possible to just reuse the username and password that you used when registering and signing up for AWS however, this is very bad practice as it grants "root" access to all of your account to whoever has those credentials. IAM allows you to create users and groups to control this access in a more secure manner. Amazon has a full explanation about why it is bad to reuse the root user as https://docs.aws.amazon.com/IAM/latest/UserGuide/best-practices.html#create-iam-users

So, let's create an Identity Access Management (IAM) user.

Navigate to the AWS console at https://eu-west-2.console.aws.amazon.com/console/home

Enter "IAM" in the **Find services** box.

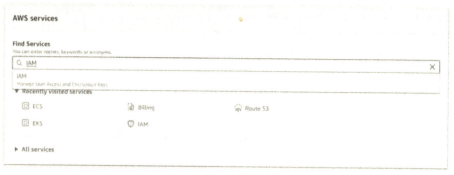

9 - AWS Find services form

Choose the IAM link that pops up. This will show the IAM section. On the left click "Users" and then on the "Add User" button.

Set user details

You can add multiple users at once with the same access type and permissions. Learn more

User name* [   ]

⊕ Add another user

Select AWS access type

Select how these users will access AWS. Access keys and autogenerated passwords are provided in the last step. Learn more

Access type* ✔ **Programmatic access**
Enables an **access key ID** and **secret access key** for the AWS API, CLI, SDK, and other development tools.

☐ **AWS Management Console access**
Enables a **password** that allows users to sign-in to the AWS Management Console.

10 - AWS Add user form

Note: That we require programmatic access for this user.

Enter the username (for example, I have used jenkinsUser).

Click "Next: Permissions"

We now want to create a group so that we can control access to our resources. Click "Create group"

Enter a name for the group. Then we need to pick the appropriate permissions to grant on this role.

In the Filter policies box enter "EC2"

Filter policies ⌄	Q EC2		
Policy name ⌄		**Type**	**Used as**
▸ 🗃 AmazonEC2ContainerRegistryFullAccess		AWS managed	None
▸ 🗃 AmazonEC2ContainerRegistryPowerUser		AWS managed	None
▸ 🗃 AmazonEC2ContainerRegistryReadOnly		AWS managed	None
▸ 🗃 AmazonEC2ContainerServiceAutoscaleRole		AWS managed	None
▸ 🗃 AmazonEC2ContainerServiceEventsRole		AWS managed	None
▸ 🗃 AmazonEC2ContainerServiceforEC2Role		AWS managed	None
▸ 🗃 AmazonEC2ContainerServiceFullAccess		AWS managed	None
▸ 🗃 AmazonEC2ContainerServiceRole		AWS managed	None
▸ 🗃 AmazonEC2FullAccess		AWS managed	None
▸ 🗃 AmazonEC2ReadOnlyAccess		AWS managed	None

11 - AWS filtering policies

We can now click on the checkbox next to "AmazonEC2ContainerRegistryPowerUser" to mark it as selected.

We need to create the virtual server which will host our Jenkins server instance. We will use the free tier eligible options for this service.

Navigate to the AWS console https://aws.amazon.com/console/home

Then in the Find services search enter "EC2". Choose the EC2 link.

This takes you to the EC2 console. In the middle click the "Launch Instance" button

We are going to create an "Amazon Linux 2 AMI" instance. This is free eligible at the time of writing. For a list of the free tier resources available to you now go to https://aws.amazon.com/free/?all-free-tier.sort-by=item.additionalFields.SortRank&all-free-tier.sort-order=asc

Find it from the list (usually at the top) or enter "Amazon Linux 2 AMI" in the filter then click "select".

We now need to pick the resources that will be allocated to the instance, select "t2.micro" from this list, again this is the free tier eligible choice at the time of writing. Then click "Review and Launch" this then allows you to review the configuration.

We need to enable access to our Jenkins server so we want to click on "Edit security groups"

Then click "Add rule" this allows us to enter the information about what we are accepting connections. In the "Type" drop-down select HTTPS, then click "Review and Launch".

There will be a warning about security, we can safely ignore this for the moment.

Now we can click "Launch".

We are now required to provide some access keys to allow access to the EC2 instance once it is started.

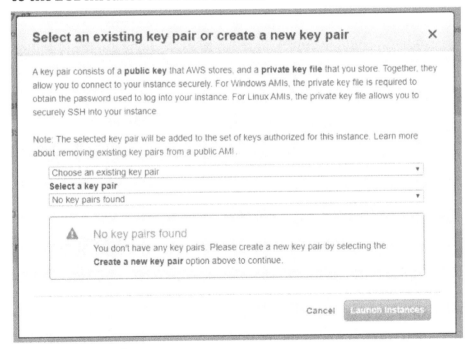

12 - AWS Configure keys

Choose "Create new key pair" then provide a name for the generated pair. For example, "JenkinsAWSKeys".

Click "Download Key Pair" which will download a "PEM" file to your local device, once this has completed click "Launch Instances"

The "PEM" file or "Privacy enhanced mail" file is a security certificate file that should be kept private to you, this is because it is the authentication certificate which grants access to the EC2 instance we are creating. Although we are not going to use it in this book, if you prefer to connect using SSH instead of the Browser connections (see below), then you will require this file.

You can click "View Instances" to see how your instance is coming along. Once the instance is running, which is shown in the fourth tab, we can connect to the instance.

Ensure that the instance is selected on the left-hand check box then click "Connect"

Connect To Your Instance   ✕

I would like to connect with   ○ A standalone SSH client ⓘ
                                    ◉ EC2 Instance Connect (browser-based SSH connection) ⓘ
                                    ○ A Java SSH Client directly from my browser (Java required) ⓘ

Connect using a custom user name, or default to the user name for the AMI used to launch the instance. Learn more

         User name | ec2-user | ⓘ

                                                              [Close] [Connect]

13 - AWS SSH connection

Choose "EC2 Instance Connect (browser-based SSH connection)" and then leave the User name as is.

Click "Connect". This will create a Linux terminal session for you to interact with the VM.

Now that we have our terminal we can begin installing the various services that we require.

First up, we will install NginX. NginX is a compact web server which is often used as a "reverse proxy" to handle routing incoming requests correctly. We are going to use this to allow us to forward requests into our Jenkins server.

In the terminal, type in "sudo amazon-linux-extras install nginx1" and hit enter. This will kick off the NginX install process.

```
Package                        Arch    Version                  Repository            Size
=========================================================================================
Installing:
 nginx                         x86_64  1:1.12.2-2.amzn2.0.2     amzn2extra-nginx1     533 k
Installing for dependencies:
 fontconfig                    x86_64  2.10.95-11.amzn2.0.2     amzn2-core            231 k
 fontpackages-filesystem       noarch  1.44-8.amzn2             amzn2-core             10 k
 gd                            x86_64  2.0.35-26.amzn2.0.2      amzn2-core            147 k
 gperftools-libs               x86_64  2.6.1-1.amzn2            amzn2-core            274 k
 libX11                        x86_64  1.6.5-2.amzn2.0.2        amzn2-core            614 k
 libX11-common                 noarch  1.6.5-2.amzn2.0.2        amzn2-core            164 k
 libXau                        x86_64  1.0.8-2.1.amzn2.0.2      amzn2-core             29 k
 libXpm                        x86_64  3.5.12-1.amzn2.0.2       amzn2-core             57 k
 libpng                        x86_64  2:1.5.13-7.amzn2.0.2     amzn2-core            214 k
 libxcb                        x86_64  1.12-1.amzn2.0.2         amzn2-core            216 k
 libxslt                       x86_64  1.1.28-5.amzn2.0.2       amzn2-core            243 k
 nginx-all-modules             noarch  1:1.12.2-2.amzn2.0.2     amzn2extra-nginx1      17 k
 nginx-filesystem              noarch  1:1.12.2-2.amzn2.0.2     amzn2extra-nginx1      17 k
 nginx-mod-http-geoip          x86_64  1:1.12.2-2.amzn2.0.2     amzn2extra-nginx1      24 k
 nginx-mod-http-image-filter   x86_64  1:1.12.2-2.amzn2.0.2     amzn2extra-nginx1      27 k
 nginx-mod-http-perl           x86_64  1:1.12.2-2.amzn2.0.2     amzn2extra-nginx1      37 k
 nginx-mod-http-xslt-filter    x86_64  1:1.12.2-2.amzn2.0.2     amzn2extra-nginx1      26 k
 nginx-mod-mail                x86_64  1:1.12.2-2.amzn2.0.2     amzn2extra-nginx1      55 k
 nginx-mod-stream              x86_64  1:1.12.2-2.amzn2.0.2     amzn2extra-nginx1      76 k
 stix-fonts                    noarch  1.1.0-5.amzn2            amzn2-core            1.3 M

Transaction Summary
=========================================================================================
Install  1 Package (+20 Dependent packages)

Total download size: 4.2 M
Installed size: 11 M
Is this ok [y/d/N]: 
```

14 - NginX install confirmation

Enter "y" and hit enter to finish installing NginX.

Next we need to ensure that Git and Java are installed. These are used by Jenkins.

Type "sudo yum install -y git java-11-amazon-corretto" and hit enter

Now we need to install the Jenkins server. First let's ensure that we have the latest version of the OS installed. Enter "sudo yum update –y" and press enter. The "-y" switch at the end saves us having the review the artifacts prior to install.

We will also need to install git. Type "sudo yum install -y git"

We then need to ensure we have an appropriate version of java installed. Type "sudo yum install -y java-11-amazon-corretto-headless" and hit enter.

Now type in "sudo wget -O /etc/yum.repos.d/jenkins.repo https://pkg.jenkins.io/redhat/jenkins.repo" and press enter. This will ensure that we are using the Jenkins yum repo. To go with this we want to obtain the key for the repo. This will reduce the likelihood of us getting malicious code rather than our expected applications / utilities.

Type in "sudo rpm --import https://pkg.jenkins.io/redhat/jenkins.io.key" and, again, press enter. Now we have the Jenkins repository all setup we can go ahead and install the server. Type in "sudo yum install Jenkins -y" followed by enter.

CONFIGURING NGINX TO ROUTE TO JENKINS

Before we actually start up our Jenkins server, we need to configure the NginX service to route traffic through to the Jenkins server. This will ensure that HTTP traffic between GitHub and Jenkins is encrypted. This will also ensure that any HTTP traffic is encrypted as well.

Obtaining a fully signed certificate is beyond the scope of this book, but we will create a self-signed certificate to get us up and running.

OK, let's configure the NginX service. First, we will need to open a console to our EC2 instance. See the previous chapter for details if you do not already have the console open.

We need to obtain our hostname so type in "hostname" and hit enter. Remember the response as we will need it in a moment.

We will also need to know the public DNS assigned by AWS. This is shown in the EC2 UI under the "Public DNS (IPv4)"

This will be something like"ec2-99-123-99-9.region.compute.amazonaws.com"

We will use the built in text editor **vi** to configure the various required files for this section. You can easily switch out **vi** for **nano** if this is more comfortable for you to use.

Run "sudo vi /etc/nginx/conf.d/jenkins.conf" from the terminal.

Press "i" to enter insert mode then enter the following configuration into the Jenkins.conf file:

```
server {
    listen 80;
    server_name <hostname for the ec2 instance>;
    return 301 https://$host$request_uri;
}

server {
    listen 443 ssl;
    server_name <hostname for the EC2 instance>;
    ssl_certificate/etc/nginx/cert.crt;
    ssl_certificate_key/etc/nginx/cert.key;

ssl on;
    ssl_session_cache builtin:1000 shared:SSL:10m;
    ssl_protocols TLSv1.1 TLSv1.2;
    ssl_ciphers HIGH:!aNULL:!eNULL:!EXPORT:!CAMELLIA:!DES:!MD5:!PSK:!RC4;
    ssl_prefer_server_ciphers on;
access_log/var/log/nginx/jenkins.access.log;

location / {
proxy_set_headerHost $host;
proxy_set_headerX-Real-IP $remote_addr;
proxy_set_headerX-Forwarded-For $proxy_add_x_forwarded_for;
proxy_set_headerX-Forwarded-Proto $scheme;
proxy_passhttp://localhost:8080;
proxy_read_timeout 90;
proxy_redirect    <Public DNS (IPv4)>;
    }
}
```

Once that is in press **esc** and then enter ":x" to save and quit the editor.

Now we need to generate a self signed certificate for NginX to use. To do this we need to become the root user. This has some risk associated with it as, the root user has all rights and privileges on the virtual machine. Generally it is better to prepend "sudo" to an individual command to limit this risk. In this case we have several steps to perform so becoming root for a short period is more efficient.

Type "sudo -sH" and enter to become root, then type "cd /etc/nginx" and enter to change directories to the NginX config directory.

Type "yum install -y mod_ssl" and press enter.

This will install a script to help setup our certificates

Now type "/etc/pki/tls/certs/make-dummy-cert cert.certificate" and hit enter

This will generate a self-signed certificate. It stores both the public and private part in the file so we need to split it into cert.key for the private part and cert.crt for the public part.

Type "cat cert.certificate" then hit enter.

This will now output the certificate that we generated to our console.

Highlight from "-----BEGIN PRIVATE KEY-----" until "-----END PRIVATE KEY-----" then copy this.

Type "vi cert.key" and press enter

Type "i" and then paste the private key contents into the editor.

Press **esc** and then type ":x" and press enter.

Type "cat cert.certificate" again and hit enter.

This time highlight from "-----BEGIN CERTIFICATE-----" and "-----END CERTIFICATE-----"

Type "vi cert.crt" press enter and then "i"

Paste in the certificate.

```
-----BEGIN CERTIFICATE-----
MIIESzCCAzOgAwIBAgIJAIkWxGdRdoh/MAOGCSqGSIb3DQEBCwUAMIG7MQswCQYD
VQQGEwItLTESMBAGA1UECAwJU29tZVNOYXRlMREwDwYDVQQHDAhTb211021OeTEZ
MBcGA1UECgwQU29tZU9yZ2FuaXphdGlvbjEfMB0GA1UECwwWU29tZU9yZ2FuaXph
dGlvbmFsVW5pdDEeMBwGA1UEAwwVbG9jYWxob3NOLmxvY2FsZG9tYWluMSkwJwYJ
KoZIhvcNAQkBFhpyb290QGxvY2FsaG9zdC5sb2NhbGRvbWFpbjAeFw0xOTEwMDQx
NTIONDhaFw0yMDEwMDMxNTIONDhaMIG7MQswCQYDVQQGEwItLTESMBAGA1UECAwJ
U29tZVNOYXRlMREwDwYDVQQHDAhTb211021OeTEZMBcGA1UECgwQU29tZU9yZ2Fu
aXphdGlvbjEfMB0GA1UECwwWU29tZU9yZ2FuaXphdGlvbmFsVW5pdDEeMBwGA1UE
AwwVbG9jYWxob3NOLmxvY2FsZG9tYWluMSkwJwYJKoZIhvcNAQkBFhpyb290QGxv
Y2FsaG9zdC5sb2NhbGRvbWFpbjCCASIwDQYJKoZIhvcNAQEBBQADggEPADCCAQoC
ggEBAN5e9fXp+A4dry7mrKnWynFr9wydsJclFIP4Y0ICQBv4TB1N8WLA9kzYW4ot
7YvoJ+cgoez6UatYfIimGc//5h8Dhu46K3GX84UvXmNfDLa4FgtenPm8iX5CD/94
oScU+MCKwC1NN3yAgOMHsE8gOSZfr95g/JROsQ65MvngI1CONX/NEGxyVL58y7Pf
04NjUe2bgKZquvy+0PmOK61V02a4y7DkWbA3j6MmE6BLXVcSNupkUzFijfvZ/PaT
zl652+xzjvHmQZ3asF8EOxicDL862UBJ/NssEZ9/ANZvNZnfMq2+dvPevl1OFOPe
ZWCdtQGAEXkWhfCZTgbSPspAacUCAwEAAaNQME4wHQYDVROOBBYEFMZPbut4rcO2
QgzLgWMUJxvYBQz6MB8GA1UdIwQYMBaAFMZPbut4rcO2QgzLgWMUJxvYBQz6MAwG
A1UdEwQFMAMBAf8wDQYJKoZIhvcNAQELBQADggEBAM4eGlVEjql+9VIrA/eTmg0i
BspQNJiNQfONrKdr4ta5n/hygJwEOQaXs4yTMUnI3QVPWbDpeDxhj00/vRJiLBjK
KH/XcTpcqOAohY6wdIuaJZLlyvwbWmLSEEN1pJYWZ5dD2P3BEi8u7sb8BS+9GaZP
S36BUKbOrRY+xPsnpHf7Tc6CJiKvr8ibVbLwxcRO411TV2p25ojQGold/Lzg94XZ
ZlZj3Qd5C9/LpUdg4ndPsdyJSkA3rXbXLH9tV2AMHJ8sM/CkWLZR/LX1bmXLXeOE
KL7xb1dXtC9d58SUm/k/TYdBLyg0nbTN8z5GenjEUfVjVFWnShbkyivFJM6jf0s=
-----END CERTIFICATE-----
```

15 - Example cert.crt file

Press **esc** and then type ":x" and press enter.

Now we just need to start the services and we can then move on to configuring Jenkins.

Type "systemctl restart nginx Jenkins" and press enter.

This should complete with no errors.

Now we can ensure that NginX restarts whenever we start the server.

Type "systemctl enable nginx" and press enter.

Finally, we need to exit the root shell and ensure we are out of harms way. Type "logout" and press enter.

Next, let's test the installation. Open a new tab / window in your browser and navigate to https://<your public DNS>

For example, whilst writing this book, my Jenkins address is: https://ec2-35-178-16-8.eu-west-2.compute.amazonaws.com

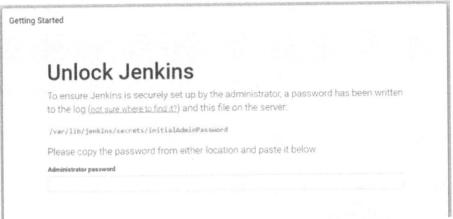

16 - Initial Jenkins screen

You should see the following screen when you navigate to the Jenkins address above. Jenkins has written a one-time password for you to use. This is done to stop anyone using the instance until it has been configured. We will go on and configure our instance in the next chapter.

CONFIGURING JENKINS

Jenkins allows for many varied configurations, so going through every option is beyond the scope of this book. We will simply be doing the minimum to get our code building and deploying.

Let's start by doing some initial setup.

First, we need to find out what our admin password is. To do this we need to open the console on to our EC2 instance. Follow the steps from the previous chapter if you have closed your console.

From within the console type "sudo cat /var/lib/jenkins/secrets/initialAdminPassword" and press enter.

This will write out the admin password to the console for you. Copy this and then we can paste it into the appropriate box on the web UI.

Do this now.

Customize Jenkins

Plugins extend Jenkins with additional features to support many different needs.

Install suggested plugins	**Select plugins to install**
Install plugins the Jenkins community finds most useful.	Select and install plugins most suitable for your needs.

17 - Jenkins plugin setup

You will be asked whether you want the suggested plugins installed or if you want to select your own.

One of the best practices for Jenkins is to try and limit the number of plugins to only those required. Also, when it comes to plugins, you want to be cautious about how many plugins you use. Plugins are often fragile and can fail. You don't want to install too many and run the risk of information getting deleted due to one failing.

Having said that, let's click "Select plugins to install"

This will open a dialog with a large number of plugins. Click "suggested" at the top to make sure the suggested plugins are initially selected.

Then do the following:

- Select the "NodeJs" plugin
- Select the HTML Publisher plugin
- Select the xUnit plugin
- Unselect the subversion plugin

Now click "Install"

The install process will take a couple of minutes, so now might be a good time for a well-earned coffee.

Once the install completes you will be prompted to add some admin user details.

Create First Admin User

Username:		
Password:		
Confirm password:		
Full name:		
E-mail address:		

18 - Jenkins admin user

Fill out the details and then click "Save and Continue"

You will then be asked to enter the root URL for Jenkins; this can be left as is. Click "Save and Finish"

Jenkins is now ready so click through and you will have the home screen of Jenkins ready to setup.

Click "Manage Jenkins" which is on the left hand side of the UI.

You can configure the Jenkins server to have various settings enabled. One of these is the email notifications. For this you will need to use the details of your email provider. I would recommend using the Amazon SES service (Simple Email Service) but configuring it is beyond the scope of the book, so is left as an exercise for the reader. You can get started though by going to https://docs.aws.amazon.com/ses/latest/DeveloperGuide/setting-up-email.html

Once you have entered this information (if required) click "Save"

Click "Manage Jenkins" again and this time click "Global Tool Configuration"

We now need to configure our tool locations.

First click on the "Install automatically" checkbox in the "Git" section.

Then click on "Add NodeJS"

19 - Jenkins NodeJS setup

Enter a name in the name box (for example, nodeJs)

Ensure that "Install Automatically" is selected

Now click on "Add Docker"

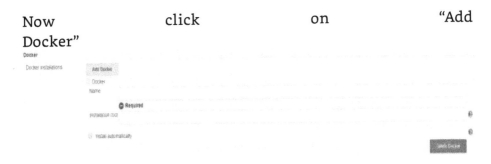

20 - Jenkins Docker setup

Again, add a name and make sure that "Install Automatically" is selected.

Click "Save"

Let's have a quick check that these are working.

Click "New Item" on the left side

21 - Jenkins New item

Enter the name "node-test" for this job.

Then click "Pipeline" and click "OK"

Then when the new job is created. Scroll down to the "Pipeline" section and enter the following into the "Script" edit:

pipeline {

  agent any

```
tools {nodejs "nodeJs"}

stages {
  stage('Example') {
    steps {
      sh 'npm config ls'
    }
  }
}
}
```

Note: the line tools {nodejs "nodeJs"} assumes that you called the NodeJS configuration "nodeJs" in the previous steps.

Click "Save"

Now click "Build Now" from the left side.

You will see the "Build History" section will have a progress bar now as the build progresses.

You should then see a blue ball appear there.

Excellent, that means we have successfully installed NodeJS and ran a simple pipeline.

We are now ready to get our code building.

Typically, you would now setup some Jenkins slaves to do the actual building and let the Server only be responsible for interacting with users and orchestrating builds. For brevity though, we are going to stick to a single instance performing all steps.

CREATING A BUILD JOB FOR OUR PROJECT

We now have our Jenkins server running, so let's get our code building and testing.

On the Jenkins UI click "New Item"

Enter an item name, for example, "javascript-on-aws". Then click "Pipeline" and then click "Save"

On the Item configuration screen, select "GitHub Project" then enter the url for the repository in the edit box.

For me this is https://github.com/shanepreater/javascript-on-aws

After this select "GitHub hook trigger for GITScm polling" from the "Build Triggers" section.

We will now be able to configure our GitHub repository to send build requests to Jenkins.

Next we need to scroll down to the "Pipeline" section. This time we want to choose "Pipeline script from SCM". This will allow us to tailor the pipeline on a per project basis. Also it allows us to pull the code from GitHub.

Next, choose "Git" from the "SCM" drop down.

This will now prompt us for the repository to use, it also allows us to add some credentials.

For a public repository on GitHub, no credentials are needed so this can be ignored.

For the repository, we want to use the same URL as we get when we click the "Clone or download" button over on GitHub. As a quick cheat this is the public repository URL appended with ".git"

So, in my example this is: https://github.com/shanepreater/javascript-on-aws.git

Leave the "" section as the default "Jenkinsfile"

Jenkins will now pull down the latest code when a build is triggered.

Click on "Save" and we are ready to test our build.

But, first, what is this Jenkinsfile that was mentioned? This is the same pipeline Groovy script that we used in the previous section to check we had Jenkins configured correctly, however instead of us defining this script in the build job, we store it alongside our code. This means that changes to the build process can be checked in with the code it builds. It also means that peer reviews and tests can be performed to ensure it works as expected. Another advantage is that it then gets "backed up" to the GitHub repository so, if you need to migrate to a new Jenkins Server or the server is rebuilt then the build process isnt' lost. The "Jenkinsfile" should be located in the route of the source code repository.

CONTINUOUS DELIVERY WITH AWS AND JAVASCRIPT

As an example, one for our code you can use:

```groovy
#!groovy
pipeline {
  agent any

  tools {nodejs "nodeJs"}

  stages {
    stage('Setup') {
      steps {
        sh 'npm install'
      }
    }
    stage('Test') {
      steps {
        sh 'npm run test:once'
      }
    }
    stage ('Build') {
      steps {
        sh 'npm run build'
      }
    }
    stage('Deploy') {
      steps {
        echo 'Deploying....'
      }
    }
  }
}
```

This will build the code and then run the tests for us. **Note:** we haven't yet hooked in the deploy step.

The other item to note in the Jenkinsfile configuration is the test stage. If you are using the create-react-app as your base then it will hook up the "npm test" command to trigger a watcher. This stays running and automatically re-runs tests as you develop. That's a good thing while developing, however, when Jenkins trys to build, if you just run the npm test then your build will never finish.

To solve this, we need to add an environment variable to the Jenkins server.

From your browser navigate to the Jenkins server.

Then click on "Manage Jenkins" on the left hand side.

Then click "Configure system" and look for the "Environment variables" checkbox in the "Global properties section"

Ensure this is checked and then in name type "CI" and in value type "true"

Click "Save".

This will ensure that the test runs just once while being run by Jenkins.

Ensure that this is committed to your repository, then we can manually run the build to test that it works.

On the Jenkins UI click the "Build Now" link. Sit back and relax whilst your code is built and tested for you.

The final step is now to get the build to be triggered by GitHub when a new commit is received.

Head over to your GitHub repository. Then on the top right click "Settings", this is next to "Insights".

Click that and you will be taken to the settings for the repository

22 - GitHub Repository settings

Click on "Webhooks", and then, "Add Webhook"

In "Payload URL" you need to enter the URL for Jenkins and add "/github-webhook/" to the end:

In my example this is https://ec2-35-178-16-8.eu-west-2.compute.amazonaws.com/github-webhook/

As we are using our own self signed certificate so click on "Disable" under the SSL verification. This will give a warning as it is less secure, it is ok to ignore this for now.

Finally ensure that "Just push the event" is selected in the "Which events would you like to trigger this webhook?" section and then click "Update webhook".

We should now have builds kick off whenever new changes are committed to the repository.

CREATING THE SONARQUBE SERVER

In case you didn't know, SonarQube is Open Source Software. SonarQube performs static code scanning which not only discovers potential vulnerabilities, but also highlights potential bugs and code smells.

What are code smells? These are sections of code which are less well formed and, although not necessarily a bug, certainly impact the quality of the code.

Warning due to the memory requirements that SonarQube needs, this is not a free tier EC2 virtual machine. SonarQube requires a minimum of 2Gb of memory for the server itself but also an additional 1Gb for the OS. This means we need a minimum of 3Gb of RAM. The closest offering that AWS offers is the "t2.medium" instance, unfortunately, this is not a free tier offering so you are welcome to skip the SonarQube setup if you do not want to incur any costs. I would recommend that you carry on and add SonarQube to your build though because of the great benefits that the code analysis provides.

First job is to create the virtual server that will host our SonarQube instance This is a very similar process to the Jenkins server setup we did previously.

As a quick recap these are the main steps (For full details see HOW TO INSTALL JENKINS ON EC2):

1. From the AWS console (https://aws.amazon.com/console/home), search for "EC2)

2. Launch a new instance and create an "Amazon Linux 2 AMI" instance.
3. Select the "t2.medium" resource. Note: This is the change from the Jenkins setup.
4. Setup the security group.
5. Add a rule to allow https connections
6. Launch the instance
7. Get the access keys. In this case you can reuse the ones created for Jenkins, or use a new pair. If you use a new pair don't forget to download the PEM file.
8. Click "View launched instance"
9. Connect to the instance.

Next we need to install the appropriate services to allow us to connect from Jenkins to this instance.

Install NginX:

Type "sudo amazon-linux-extras install nginx1" and hit enter.

Then run "sudo vi /etc/nginx/conf.d/sonarqube.conf" from the terminal.

Enter the following configuration to hook up the NginX reverse proxy with our SonarQube instance:

```
server {
listen 80;
   server_name ip-172-31-44-8.eu-west-2.compute.internal;
   access_log /var/log/nginx/sonarqube.access.log;

   location / {
     proxy_set_header Host $host;
     proxy_set_header X-Real-IP $remote_addr;
     proxy_set_header X-Forwarded-For $proxy_add_x_forwarded_for;
     proxy_set_header X-Forwarded-Proto $scheme;
     proxy_pass http://localhost:9000;
     proxy_read_timeout 150;
     proxy_redirect      http://127.0.0.1:9000      http://ec2-3-8-198-155.eu-west-2.compute.amazonaws.com/sonarqube;
   }
}

server {
  listen 443 ssl;
  server_name ip-172-31-44-8.eu-west-2.compute.internal;
  ssl_certificate /etc/nginx/cert.crt;
  ssl_certificate_key /etc/nginx/cert.key;

  ssl on;

  ssl_session_cache builtin:1000 shared:SSL:10m;
  ssl_protocols TLSv1.1 TLSv1.2;
  ssl_ciphers HIGH:!aNULL:!eNULL:!EXPORT:!CAMELLIA:!DES:!MD5:!PSK:!RC4;
  ssl_prefer_server_ciphers on;
  access_log /var/log/nginx/sonarqube.access.log;
```

```
location / {
    proxy_set_header Host $host;
    proxy_set_header X-Real-IP $remote_addr;
    proxy_set_header X-Forwarded-For $proxy_add_x_forwarded_for;
    proxy_set_header X-Forwarded-Proto $scheme;
    proxy_pass http://localhost:9000;
    proxy_read_timeout 150;
    proxy_redirect    http://127.0.0.1:9000    https://ec2-3-8-198-155.eu-west-2.compute.amazonaws.com;
  }
}
```

Hit esc and then enter ":x" to save and quit.

We are going to be using the sonarqube scanner to perform the code scanning, unfortunately this does not have a way to ignore certificate verification. This gives us two options:

1. Our SonarQube server needs to fully signed certificate
2. We need to allow HTTP access to our server.

In this book we are going to use option 2. This means we need to use the above configuration and then we need to make a small change to the main NginX configuration file.

In the terminal:

Type "sudo vi /etc/nginx/nginx.conf" and press enter.

We need to find the "server" section in the file. Delete this from "server {" until the closing "}". Then save the changes. This removed the default server configuration so that sonarqube can be served through port 80.

There are a few additional services we need in order to get SonarQube running. Let's get them installed now.

First up is Java. This is the same as with Jenkins

Type "sudo yum install -y git java-11-amazon-corretto" and hit enter

Now we can install the SonarQube server.

Type "wget https://binaries.sonarsource.com/Distribution/sonarqube/sonarqube-7.9.zip" then hit enter.

Type "sudo unzip sonarqube-7.9.zip -d /opt/" and, again, hit enter

As SonarQube uses ElasticSearch, and ElasticSearch cannot be run as root, we need to setup a sonarqube user and group.

Type "sudo groupadd sonar" then enter.

Type "sudo useradd -c "Sonar User" -d /opt/sonarqube-7.9/ -g sonar -s /bin/bash sonar" then enter.

Type "sudo chown -R sonar:sonar /opt/sonarqube-7.9" hit enter.

Now we have Sonar setup we can create a systemctl entry to ensure it starts whenever the virtual machine is started.

Type "sudo vi /etc/systemd/system/sonarqube.service" then press "i"

Copy the following configuration into the file:

[Unit]

Description=SonarQube service

After=syslog.target network.target

[Service]

Type=simple

User=sonar

Group=sonar

PermissionsStartOnly=true

ExecStart=/bin/nohup /bin/java -Xms1024m -Xmx2048m -Djava.net.preferIPv4Stack=true -jar /opt/sonarqube-7.9/lib/sonar-application-7.9.jar

StandardOutput=syslog

LimitNOFILE=65536

LimitNPROC=8192

TimeoutStartSec=5

Restart=always

[Install]

WantedBy=multi-user.target

Then press esc and ":x" followed by enter to save and quit.

Reload the system control daemon:

Type "systemctl daemon-reload" and hit enter.

Start up and enable the sonarqube service:

Type "systemctl enable sonarqube" and then press enter.

Type "systemctl restart sonarqube" and press enter.

You should now have SonarQube running. Open your browser and then navigate to "http://<public DNS>/" and you should see the SonarQube home page:

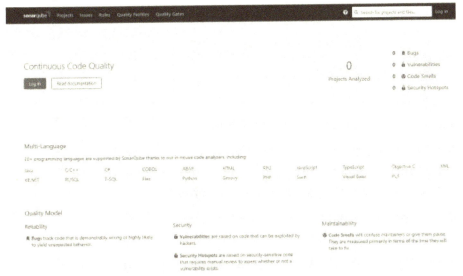

Figure 23 - SonarQube home

ADDING SONARQUBE
TO OUR PROJECT

Now that we have the sonarqube server installed and running, we need to enable sonarqube within our JavaScript project. This will allow us to get SonarQube to inspect our code and also Jenkins to integrate with it.

Open a terminal and navigate to the home directory of our JavaScript project (This is the directory that contains the package.json file).

Now type "vi sonar-scanner.properties" and press enter.

Press "i" and copy the following into the file:

sonar.projectKey=react:JSOnAWS

sonar.projectName=JavascriptOnAWS

sonar.projectVersion=1.0

sonar.sources=src/

sonar.host.url=http://<Public DNS>

We are going to use the sonar scanner to kick off the code scanning for our project. This means we need to have sonar scanner installed. We are going to use npm to achieve this.

From the terminal navigate to the home directory of the project once more.

Type "npm install sonar-scanner –save-dev" and press enter.

This will now install the scanner for the project.

We can then add a convenient script to our build system to kick off the scanning.

Open "package.json" and locate the "scripts" section. Add the following after the "test" line:

"sonar": "sonar-scanner",

That will allow us to then run "npm run sonar" from the terminal.

A code analysis should now be performed by SonarQube.

In your browser navigate to the SonarQube instance. For my example this is http://ec2-3-8-198-155.eu-west-2.compute.amazonaws.com/

Figure 24 - SonarQube with the first analysis

As you can see we now have a project that has been analyzed (top right) clicking that will show us the summary of the analysis.

Figure 25 - Analysis summary

HOW TO INTEGRATE JENKINS WITH SONARQUBE

In this chapter, we are going to go through how you can use SonarQube with Jenkins. The great thing about coding is being able to use different applications to better achieve what you are hoping to implement. With open source systems, you can play around and create. Whether you are a beginner or an expert, it is always worth looking into how to do something. That is where this chapter comes in.

When you are looking to run a SonarQube analysis in Jenkins, you are going to have to do a few steps before creating a Jenkins job.

Make sure the first thing that you do is install the SonarQube Scanner plugin. As we mentioned earlier, plugins can be tricky, but this is a necessary step in the process.

Here are the steps:

In your browser navigate to the Jenkins server.

Click on the "Manage Jenkins" option.

Click the "Manage Plugins" button.

Once you have done that then click on the "Available" view.

Look for the plugin that says "SonarQube Scanner".

Once you've clicked on this plugin then you are going to want to click the "Install without restart" option.

The last thing you need to do is wait for it to install!

Let's explore what we are going to do once everything is all installed.

Let's configure some things that are necessary on the Jenkins global configuration page.

Click on "Jenkins".

Then click on the "Manage Jenkins" options.

"Configure System" is the next thing you will click.

Then go to the "SonarQube Servers" and fill out the required details.

For name enter "sonar" and for the Server URL enter the url that we setup of the SonarQube server.

Now, we can add the sonar step into the build.

Navigate to your JavaScript code. Update the Jenkinsfile to look like this:

```groovy
#!groovy
pipeline {
  agent any

  tools {nodejs "nodeJs"}

  stages {
    stage('Setup') {
      steps {
        sh 'npm install'
      }
    }
    stage('Test') {
      steps {
        sh 'npm run test'
        withSonarQubeEnv('sonar') {
          sh "npm run sonar"
        }
      }
    }
    stage ('Build') {
      steps {
        sh 'npm run build'
      }
    }
    stage('Deploy') {
      steps {
        echo 'Deploying....'
      }
    }
```

```
    }
}
```

Commit and push the changes to GitHub. Then from your browser, navigate to the Jenkins server.

You can now build the pipeline job and you should see the SonarQube section appear in the overview.

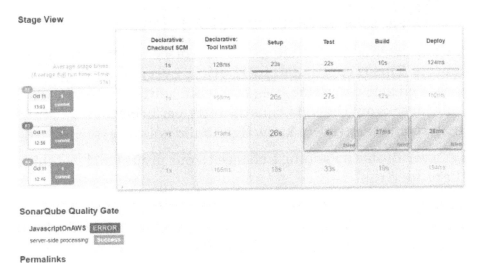

Figure 26 - Jenkins with SonarQube

The Success / Error box is a link to the report. Clicking on it will take you to the SonarQube server to see the analysis.

You will see "Passed" if all goes well, which is an extremely satisfying thing to see considering how you have worked hard on this job. You can run this in different coding languages, but SonarQube pairs perfectly with unit testing to provide the static analysis of the code. It also integrates well with Jenkins so all this information is available in one place. Our walkthrough doesn't add a check to ensure that the SonarQube analysis has passed the quality check before the build is marked as successful, but this is not difficult to add if required.

CODE CHANGE THAT INVOKES BUILD PROCESS

We now have all the building blocks in place to perform a full CI process. This is continuous integration. Every time we commit a code change to GitHub, we get a build started in Jenkins. The build checks out the code, runs the tests, performs the static code analysis and then let's us know if the build is a success.

Let's verify this by adding a change to our project and watching the process run.

Go to your code base and edit one of your files. If you are following along with the example code then you can go in and add an additional test to the project if you like.

Once you have made the change commit it and push it to GitHub. Then switch to the Jenkins server and watch the process unfold.

You can even try pushing a breaking change and verify that the build will fail.

DOCKERIZING THE APPLICATION

Now we have the process in place to continuously test and integrate our project, the final step is to get it out in front of our users. The fastest way to do this is to have Jenkins also perform continuous delivery / deployment for us as part of the build.

Let's get that working in the next two chapters. One thing worth noting though, I would recommend that only merges of pull requests to master actually fire off a deployment. This is included in the Jenkinsfile but is simple to disable if required.

OK let's decide how we are going to serve our application to our users.

With AWS, we have quite a few options to choose between. These include:

- Amplify
- Light Sail
- Elastic Beanstalk
- ECS
- Fargate
- Home rolled using EC2 instances.

If you check out my blog at https://www.shanepreater.dev/blog I have done a comparison on these different techniques to show the basic differences.

For our project we are going to deploy this to Elastic Beanstalk. The reason for this is that it is easy to setup, can be used to autonomously deploy our code and isn't only usable by JavaScript projects.

So, let's get things configured ready to automatically deploy when we get a good build.

Elastic beanstalk has a few options when it comes to deploying code. We are going to use the docker container approach in this book.

Docker is a tool built on the concept of Linux containers. This creates a virtual OS environment which acts as if it is an entire server. This means that a developer can create, deploy and run their applications with confidence that it will behave the same regardless of the underlying infrastructure that is actually used. This is because all the applications libraries, code and OS level dependencies are all packaged up together in one image to be run on that infrastructure.

We will need to create an account on https://hub.docker.com/. Open your browser and navigate to https://hub.docker.com/

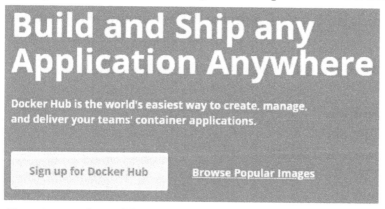

Figure 27 - Docker Hub home

Click on the "Sign up for Docker Hub" button.

You need to provide a docker ID. This is the root name for your docker images when you push them.

You also need an email and password.

Once you have created the account, we will need to generate a security token to let Jenkins push images to the docker hub.

Click on your id in the top right and on the drop down click "Account Settings"

Then on the left click "Security", then click "New Access Token"

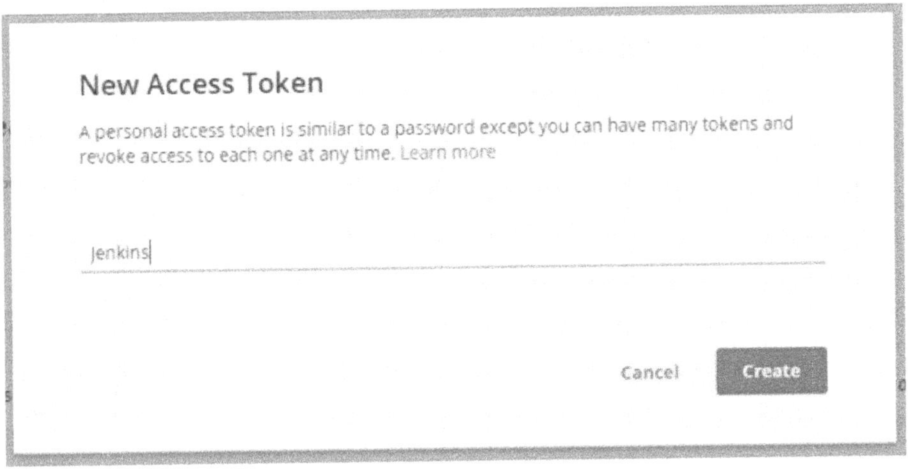

Figure 28 - Create access token

Enter the "Access token description", I used "Jenkins" in the example. This allows you to remember what you are using the access tokens for.

Click "Create". Then click "Copy and Close" The token will be copied to your clipboard.

Now navigate to your Jenkins server.

Go to "Manage Jenkins" and then "Configure Credentials" then click "Credentials" on the left.

Next click "System", then "Global" and finally "Add Credentials".

Figure 29 - Credentials for docker

Ensure "Username with password" is selected from the drop

down.

In username, type in your Docker ID

In password, paste in the access token which was generated.

In ID, type in "dockerhub"

Then click "OK"

As building our Docker image is quite memory intensive, now is a good time to spin up a slave to do that work.

Follow the steps for creating a SonarQube instance in CREATING THE SONARQUBE SERVER. We need to have Java installed on the VM.

Next, we need to install docker on the server and create a Jenkins user.

Open a console to the Jenkins slave server.

Now type "sudo yum install docker -y" then press enter.

Type "sudo adduser -b /var/lib Jenkins" then press enter.

We need to set a password for this user so we can access it via SSH, type "sudo passwd Jenkins" and press enter. Then follow the prompts to set the password.

Type "sudo usermod Jenkins -G docker" and, again, press enter.

Next, type "sudo systemctl enable docker" and press enter.

Type "sudo systemctl restart docker" and press enter.

This has installed the docker engine for use.

We now need to ensure that the Jenkins server will be able to connect to the slave. Open "/etc/ssh/ssh_config" and find the line that reads "PasswordAuthorisation no" and change it to "Password-Authorisation yes"

Save and quit the editor.

In the browser, navigate to the Jenkins server home page.

Click "Manage Jenkins" and then "Manage Nodes"

Then click "New Node". Enter a sensible name for "Node name" and ensure "Permanent Agent" is selected and then click "OK".

In "Remote root directory", type "/var/lib/Jenkins" and in the "Launch method" section ensure that "Launch agent agents via SSH" and add the public DNS for the slave VM in the "Host" field.

In the "Credentials" section click "Add", "Jenkins" and fill in the username and password with the Jenkins user details from the slave. Finally click "Add" and then select the newly created credentials in the dropdown. Finally select "Non verifying Verification Strategy" in the "Host Key Verification Strategy". Then click "Save"

This will now show the main node page with both the Server and slave shown. Click on the slave and then click "Launch Agent" to start the slave.

The final step is to stop builds from occurring on the Jenkins server. Click "Manage Jenkins" and then "Configure System" change the "# of Executors" to 0 from 1 and click "Save".

We have now setup the building blocks we need to automatically push working images to Docker Hub. Let's update our project to utilize this now.

The first step in "Dockerizing" the application is to provide docker with the details of what we want built and how we want to have it run. This is handled in a "Dockerfile" file which is Docker's equivalent of the package.json for NodeJs or the pom.xml for Maven etc.

Let's create this "Dockerfile" in the base directory alongside the package.json file with the following content:

```
FROM node:9.4

WORKDIR /app

COPY . /app

RUN npm install && npm run build

CMD npm start –production
```

EXPOSE 3000

Now we can update our "Jenkinsfile" to perform the build and deployment as part of the build sequence.

Update the Jenkinsfile like below:

```groovy
#!groovy
pipeline {
    agent any
    tools { nodejs "nodeJs"}
    environment {
        DOCKER_ID = "<Enter your Docker ID here>"
        IMAGE_NAME = "<Enter the image name here>"
    }
    stages {
        stage('Setup') {
            steps {
                sh 'npm install'
            }
        }
        stage('Test') {
            steps {
                sh 'npm run test'
                withSonarQubeEnv('sonar') {
                    sh "npm run sonar"
                }
            }
        }
        stage('Build') {
            when {
                branch 'master'
            }
            steps {
                withCredentials([usernamePassword(credentialsId: 'dockerhub', passwordVariable: 'password', usernameVariable: 'user')]) {
                    echo "Building docker image javascriptonaws:${env.BUILD_ID}"
```

```
        script {
            sh "docker login --username $user --password $password"
            echo "Login complete. Building image..."
            sh "docker build -t ${env.DOCKER_ID}/${env.IMAGE_NAME}:${env.BUILD_ID} ."
            echo "Image built. Tagging with latest"
            sh "docker tag ${env.DOCKER_ID}/${env.IMAGE_NAME}:${env.BUILD_ID} ${env.DOCKER_ID}/${env.IMAGE_NAME}:latest"
            sh "docker push ${env.DOCKER_ID}/${env.IMAGE_NAME}:${env.BUILD_ID}"
            sh "docker push ${env.DOCKER_ID}/${env.IMAGE_NAME}:latest"
            echo "Pushed with tags."
        }
      }
    }
  }
  stage('Deploy') {
    when {
      branch 'master'
    }
    steps {
      sh 'echo deploying to AWS'
    }
  }
 }
}
```

Replace the "<Enter your Docker ID here>" with your DockerHub ID and "<Enter the image name here>" with the name of the image you want to use on Docker hub. In my example I am using "javascriptonaws".

Commit and push those changes to GitHub so that it will trigger our build on Jenkins.

ENABLING CONTINUOUS DELIVERY

In this chapter we are going to leverage the fact that our Jenkins slave is an EC2 instance. Having this means that we get the AWS command line client preinstalled. We are going to make use of that to automatically deliver our software. We have two aspects of the client to make use of: "s3" this is Amazon's dynamic storage solution. It stands for simple storage service. It allows us to upload files and have them accessible to our Elastic Beanstalk application. "elasticbeanstalk" this is the client controls for managing and running Elastic Beanstalk workloads.

We need to create a simple deployment json file to allow elastic beanstalk to deploy the docker image ready for use.

Create a Dockerrun.aws.json file and then use the following content:

```
{
  "AWSEBDockerrunVersion": "1",
  "Image": {
    "Name": <Full Docker name to your image>",
    "Update": "true"
  },
  "Ports": [
    {
      "ContainerPort": "3000"
    }
  ]
```

}

Replace "<Full Docker name to your image>" with the full docker name, for example, shanepreater/javascriptonaws:45.

Then use your browser to navigate to the AWS console.

Click the services link and choose "Elastic Beanstalk" from the compute section.

This will open the Elastic Beanstalk home page. In the top right click "Create New Application"

You will then have a form to fill in

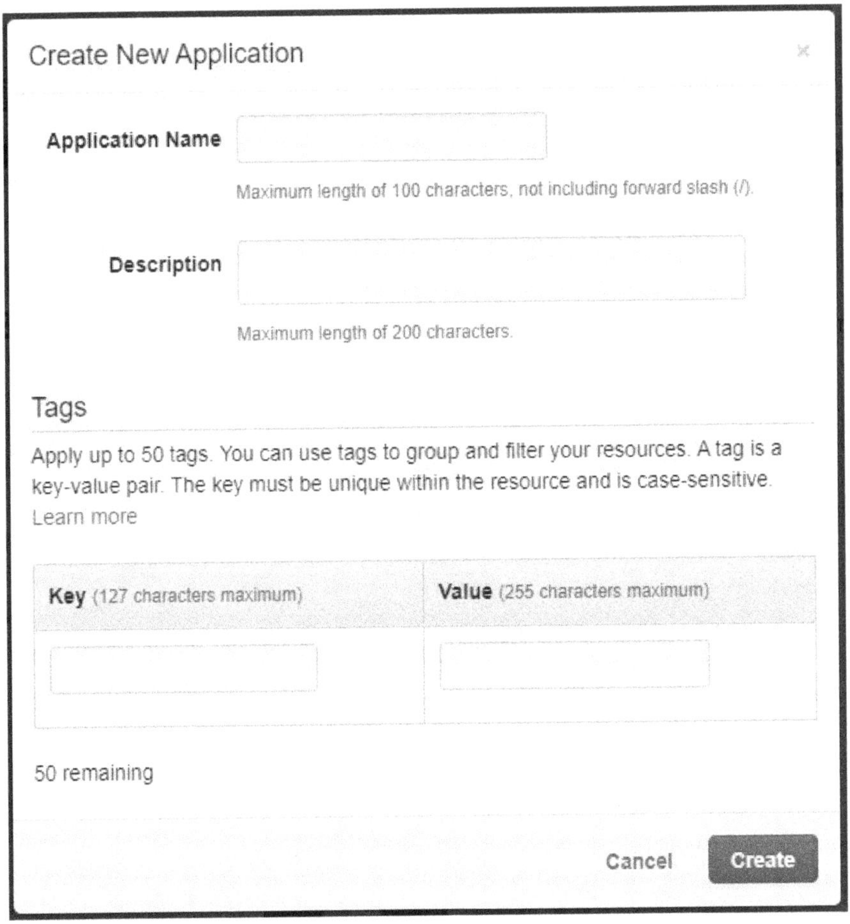

Figure 30 - Elastic Beanstalk new app

Enter the name that was used for the Docker image name in the previous chapter, and a description and then click "Create"

Figure 31 - New application screen

This will provide a new application but with no environment. Click "Create one now"

Enter

We will then have a couple of options for the type of application we are creating.

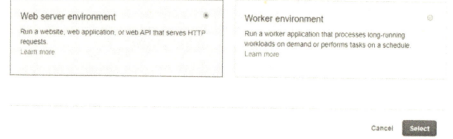

Figure 32 - Environment type

Pick "Web server environment" and click "Select".

Create a web server environment

Launch an environment with a sample application or your own code. By creating an environment, you allow AWS Elastic Beanstalk to manage AWS resources and permissions on your behalf. Learn more

Environment information

Choose the name, subdomain, and description for your environment. These cannot be changed later

Application name	javascriptonaws
Environment name	Javascriptonaws-env
Domain	enter name for subdomain value .eu-west-2.elasticbeanstalk.com Check availability
Description	

Base configuration

Platform   ● Preconfigured platform

     Platforms published and maintained by AWS Elastic Beanstalk

     -- Choose a platform --

     Custom platform

     Platforms created and owned by you. Learn more

     -- Choose a custom platform --

Application code   ● Sample application

     Get started right away with sample code

     Existing version

     Application versions that you have uploaded for bobo

     -- Choose a version --

     ○ Upload your code

     Upload a source bundle from your computer or copy one from Amazon S3.

     ⬆ Upload   ZIP or WAR

Figure 33 - Environment configuration

Enter a name for the environment, for example, staging.

Then you can optionally choose a more memorable name for the domain.

In the "Base Configuration" section choose "Docker" from the "Preconfigured platform" radio.

In "Application code" select "Existing version".

Then select the "Upload your code" radio in the "Application code" section.

Then click "Upload"

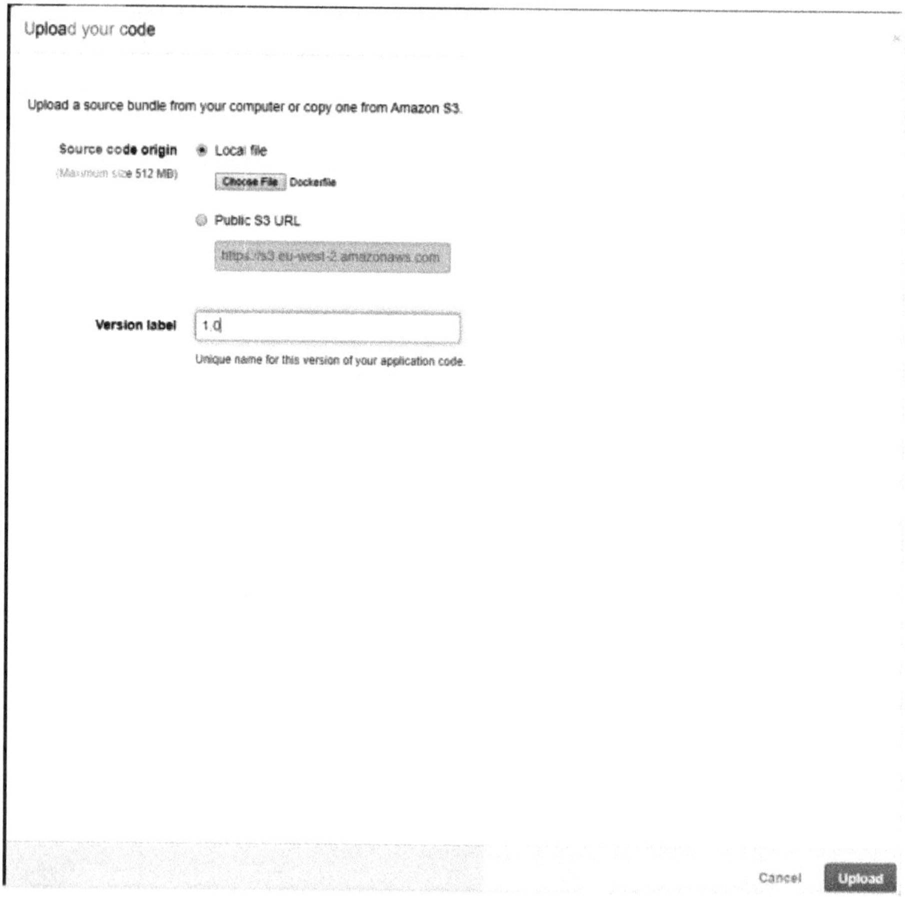

Figure 34 - Dockerfile upload screen

Choose local file and then click "Choose File"

Select the "Dokerrun.aws.json" we created previously.

Choose a "Version label" (1.0 is a good first version) then click "Upload"

It's time for another coffee as the environment setup process can take a few minutes to complete.

Once this has completed you will be given a "URL", click this to see your app running.

Now we need to hook our build into this system.

Re visit the Jenkinsfile. Add the following within the "Deploy" stage part:

```
when {
            branch 'master'
        }
        steps {
            echo 'deploying to AWS'
            echo " -> Creating the Dockerrun.aws.json file"
            writeFile file: 'Dockerrun.aws.json', text: """{
    "AWSEBDockerrunVersion": "1",
    "Image": {
      "Name": "${env.DOCKER_ID}/${env.IMAGE_NAME}:${env.BUILD_ID}",
      "Update": "true"
    },
    "Ports": [
      {
        "ContainerPort": "3000"
      }
    ]
}
"""
            echo " -> Updating the S3 bucket"
            sh "aws s3 mb s3://${env.DOCKER_ID}-${IMAGE_NAME}-${env.BUILD_ID}"

            echo " -> Uploading Dockerrun.aws.json"
            sh "aws s3 cp Dockerrun.aws.json s3://${env.DOCKER_ID}-${IMAGE_NAME}-${env.BUILD_ID}"

            echo " -> Creating application version"
            sh "aws elasticbeanstalk create-application-version --auto-create-
```

application --application-name ${env.IMAGE_NAME} --version-label v${env.BUILD_ID} --source-bundle S3Bucket=${env.DOCKER_ID}-${IMAGE_NAME}-${env.BUILD_ID},S3Key=Dockerrun.aws.json"

echo " -> Deploying new version"

sh "aws elasticbeanstalk update-application-version --application-name ${env.IMAGE_NAME} --version-label v${env.BUILD_ID}"

echo " -> Upgrading the ${env.ENVIRONMENT_NAME} with the new deployment"

sh "aws elasticbeanstalk update-environment --environment-name ${env.ENVIRONMENT_NAME} --application-name ${env.IMAGE_NAME} --version-label v${env.BUILD_ID}"

}

Notice that this uses an additional environment variable called "ENVIRONMENT_NAME" set this to the name of the newly created environment in the environment section at the top of the Jenkinsfile.

Commit and push this code. You should now have a build which automatically deploys working versions to your staging environment.

There is one more thing which is worth adding to the Jenkinsfile. After a successful build it is worth cleaning out the Docker images or you will quickly run out of space on the Jenkins slave.

To do this add an additional stage to the Jenkins file like the one below:

stage("Post build cleanup") {

steps {

echo "Cleaning up the docker images to conserve space"

sh "docker rmi -f \`docker images ${env.DOCKER_ID}/${env.IMAGE_NAME}:${env.BUILD_ID} -q\`"

}

}

This will ensure that pushed images will be cleaned from the Jenkins slave and save you space.

The fully complete Jenkinsfile can be found at https://github.com/shanepreater/javascript-on-aws/blob/master/Jenkinsfile in case you have any problems. This is configured for the example app that accompanies this book so remember to change the environment variables etc for your specific scenario.

CONCLUSION

Hopefully, as you look back at this eBook you have gained a beginner's idea of how to bring all of these services together and you are able to successfully work your project into what you had dreamt it up to be. While it may seem scary at first to think of AWS and GitHub and Jenkins along with JavaScript, everything is a learning process. There's nothing wrong with referring back to guidebooks and remember, code changes every day and what we thought was impossible yesterday becomes possible tomorrow. This is the wonderful thing about open source and why you should look into using them for your next project. There is a lot more you can do with the CI/CD pipeline that we have started here. You can scale out the slaves as you get more code / developers working on the project. You can add additional stages to the build to perform other assurance steps. You could even add social notifications when the new version is deployed so your customers are able to begin exploring the awesome new features as soon as they are ready. The choices are endless.

I hope you have found this book useful and it has given you a good starting point for using AWS and the CI/CD process, if so please leave a review on Amazon. Happy coding!